U

Insights into
Mental and Spiritual Healing
and Victory

Dan Gabbert

TEACH Services, Inc.
P U B L I S H I N G
www.TEACHServices.com • (800) 367-1844

World rights reserved. This book or any portion thereof may not be copied or reproduced in any form or manner whatever, except as provided by law, without the written permission of the publisher, except by a reviewer who may quote brief passages in a review.

The author assumes full responsibility for the accuracy of all facts and quotations as cited in this book. The opinions expressed in this book are the author's personal views and interpretations, and do not necessarily reflect those of the publisher.

This book is provided with the understanding that the publisher is not engaged in giving spiritual, legal, medical, or other professional advice. If authoritative advice is needed, the reader should seek the counsel of a competent professional.

Copyright © 2019 Dan Gabbert
Copyright © 2019 TEACH Services, Inc.
ISBN-13: 978-1-4796-1170-6 (Paperback)
ISBN-13: 978-1-4796-1171-3 (ePub)
Library of Congress Control Number: 2020902603

Gabbert, Daniel L., *Unbound! Insights into Mental and Spiritual Healing and Victory*, understanding the vital mental and spiritual components and their practical application in everyday living for three-dimensional victory and healing preparatory for an eternity of peace and rest at the return of Jesus Christ.

Unless otherwise identified, all scriptures quoted in this book are from *The Holy Bible, New King James Version*, copyright 1979, 1980, 1982, HarperCollins. Used by permission of Thomas Nelson Publishers.

Alert: All bold and italicized emphasis in this book is the author's.

TEACH Services, Inc.
P U B L I S H I N G
www.TEACHServices.com • (800) 367-1844

Foreword

For I know the thoughts that I think toward
you, … thoughts of peace and not of evil to
give you a future and a hope.
(Jeremiah 29:11)

It may seem a bit strange to you, but, whatever your circumstance, you are responding to a divine invitation to examine the evidences of a loving God and of His profound way of bringing hope, healing, and restoration to broken lives ravaged by the experiences of living in this pain-filled world.

Maybe you are wondering whether a loving God, an eternal Creator, exists. If you are inclined to think that He does not exist, consider the following thoughts before laying this book aside: **What if God does exist** and the things unfolded in this book about His way of helping hurting people are true? Think with me—if the concepts presented in this book are true and a person refuses to examine them, then by default that person will more than likely continue to experience less than his potential of peace, hope, and joy in this unsettled world of disorder, distrust, and dysfunction. More importantly, he will have lost the eternity of peace and joy, freedom from sickness, sorrow, and death that the loving Creator offers! **On the other hand, even if God does not exist**, but a person decides to examine and practice the methods of restoration presented in this book, that person will still experience, with the many others who practice these methods, some of the healing benefits these concepts of health and healing provide.

The choice is yours. Take some time to give the concepts contained herein a chance to prove their benefit to your life. It may be the beginning of an incredible journey of healing that will continue into eternity!

No matter what is hidden in your past or what is presently happening in your life, take courage! There is hope! Our loving heavenly Father, the Creator of the cosmos and of all that is true and lovely has a plan crafted just for you and your specific needs **through His empowering grace** (2 Corinthians 9:8) to bring you healing, restoration, and an incredible future—eternally filled with experiences above and beyond anything our 21st century minds can comprehend! (See 1 Corinthians 2:9, 10; Ephesians 3:20, 21.) Through His Word, the Father invites you to give Him the opportunity to unfold to your heart His healing plan, which offers everyone an open door that leads to an eternal, hope-filled future (Romans 15:4; Psalm 107:19–21; Jeremiah 29:11). I have personally commenced the journey described in this book, and I wouldn't trade it for anything!

The Author

Core Foundational Statement

(for everything contained herein)

The religion of Christ is not what many think it is, nor what their lives represent it to be. The love of God in the soul will have a direct influence upon the life, and will call the intellect and the affections into active, healthful exercise. The child of God will not rest satisfied until he is clothed with the righteousness of Christ, and sustained by His life-giving power. When he sees a weakness in his character, it is not enough to confess it again and again; he must go to work with determination and energy to overcome his defects by building up opposite traits of character. He will not shun this work because it is difficult. Untiring energy is required of the Christian; but he is not obliged to work in his own strength; divine power awaits his demand. Every one who is sincerely striving for victory over self will appropriate the promise, "My grace is sufficient for thee."

Through personal effort joined with the prayer of faith, the soul is trained. Day by day the character grows into the likeness of Christ; and finally, instead of being the sport of circumstances, instead of indulging selfishness and being carried away by light and trifling conversation, the man is master of his thoughts and words. It may cost a severe conflict to overcome habits which have been long indulged, but we may triumph through the grace of Christ. He invites us to learn of him. (Ellen G. White, *Review and Herald*, June 10, 1884; Matthew 11:28–30)

Table of Contents

Chapter One

Fuel for the Soul—
Freedom or Slavery

> *"If you abide in My word, you are My disciples indeed. And you shall know the truth, and the truth shall make you free." … "Therefore if the Son makes you free, you shall be free indeed." (John 8:31, 32, 36)*

I enjoy gifts—especially if they are useful to me. Regardless of our religious persuasion, amongst the many wonderful gifts that God has provided for our benefit, two specific spiritual gifts top the list—not because they are better in quality than any other gift, but because their use affects how much benefit a person will receive from the plethora of other gifts the Lord has provided for our protection, health, and care. Here they are: (1) the ability to believe in, to place faith in, or to trust (Romans 12:3); (2) the freedom to choose in whom or in what we are actually going to place that gift of faith, what we are going to think, and how we are going to respond to life's varied circumstances, both positive and negative (Joshua 24:15; Romans 6:16). The way these two gifts, faith and choice, are exercised in anyone's life will determine whether we experience the true healing and freedom that God wants for us, or whether we suffer the damaging slavery and entrapment that misuse of those gifts inevitably brings.

Let me explain how this works through the use of a simple illustration. Without the right kind of fuel an automobile's ability to function properly will in some way be hindered—even to the point of not running at all! Similarly, without the right kind of mental and spiritual fuel, faith and choice do not function well either. Faith (which is the ability to believe) and choice (which is the freedom to decide) are both functions of the frontal lobe of the brain, which is the heart of our mind and the seat of reason and judgment (Romans 10:10; 6:16, 17; Luke 5:22; 1 Kings 3:9). Since faith and choice are activities of the frontal lobe, the "fuel" that faith and choice require to function is *information*.

Without the right kind of fuel
an automobile's ability to function
properly will in some way be hindered—
even to the point of not running at all!
Similarly, without the right kind of mental
and spiritual fuel, faith and choice
do not function well either.

This is because our mental, spiritual, and physical well-being is directly affected by the truthfulness and healthfulness of the information that we choose to feed our minds upon through our senses, that is, through what we read, watch, and listen to.

Enter the Bible as the "informational fuel" for the mental activities of the frontal lobe, the heart of the mind. Notice the effect that God says His Word, the Bible, can have upon a person. Proverbs 4:20–22 declares:

> My son, *give attention to my words*;
> Incline your ear to my sayings.
> Do not let them depart from your eyes;
> Keep them in the midst of your heart;
> For they are *life* to those who find them,
> And *health* to all their flesh.

Did you see it? Did you catch the effect that God's Word can have upon a person? It is life and health! What kind of life and health can the Lord instill through His Word when people with a humble willing heart turn to Him for help, and by grace-empowered faith, study and practice the instructions the Bible contains concerning their physical, mental, and spiritual health? Consider the amazing life and health offered by the Lord through His Word:

> *I sought the LORD, and He heard me, and delivered me from all my fears ... This poor man cried out, and the LORD heard him, and saved him out of all his troubles ... they cried out to the LORD in their*

*trouble, and **He saved them out of their dis-tresses. <u>He sent His word</u> and healed them, and delivered them from their destructions.** (Psalm 34:4, 6; 107:19, 20)*

Being saved out of all troubles and dis-tresses, healing and deliverance from my destructions, liberation from fear—are these not all valuable benefits? I believe they are!

Why do the Scriptures have such a pro-found and healing effect upon people who decide to exercise their powers of choice and faith to contemplate and practice their instructions? It is because of the spirit and life of the Person to which they point us (John 6:63)! From front to back—from the Old Testament to the New—the Bible points us to Jesus Christ, the eternal Son of God, the One who came to earth to live and die for us to provide us a healthy model for liv-ing a happy, contented, and peaceful life—even amidst trial, conflict, persecution, and rejection (John 5:39; 14:27; 16:33).

Christ's mission statement for His sojourn on planet earth is encapsulated in Luke 4:16–19:

"The Spirit of the Lord is upon Me, because He has anointed Me to preach the gospel to the poor; He has sent Me to heal the brokenhearted, to proclaim liberty to the captives and recovery of sight to the blind, to set at liberty those who are oppressed; to proclaim the acceptable year of the Lord."

What gratitude should fill our thoughts to know that, in the challenging circumstances of our lives, the Lord has only our best interest in mind (Jeremiah 29:11)! What hope it is to know that, through His word, it is possible to experience healing from a broken heart—to be set free from the captivity of the oppression of a damaging lifestyle (John 8:31, 32)!

But here is a little frosting on the cake of happier and healthier peace-filled living—another reason the information contained in the Word of God is so vital for us:

"And this is eternal life, that they may know You, the only true God, and Jesus Christ whom You have sent." (John 17:3)

Eternal life is based upon knowing God! The Bible is the source of the information that God has given mankind to enable us to know Him as He really is—not as many people make Him out to be. And God the Father revealed His loving character through the life of Jesus Christ His Son here on earth among men. Jesus declared of Himself, *"He who sees Me sees Him who sent Me"* (John 12:45). Through His Son Jesus Christ, the mighty God of all creation and re-creation has given us His Holy Spirit-inspired Word, the Bible, and has provided us the opportunity to exercise faith and the power of choice to learn His healing ways of caring for our body and mind to prepare us to enjoy eternity in an environment free from sadness and sorrow—unencumbered by sickness, pain, and death! (See Revelation 21:3, 4.) I like that, don't you? Will you give the Lord the opportunity to prove the truthfulness of His promises?

Further Inspired Insight

Faith is the gift of God, but the power to exercise it is ours. (*Patriarchs and Prophets*, p. 431)

As a means of intellectual training, the Bible is more effective than any other book, or all other books combined. (*Education*, p. 124)

The true principles of psychology are found in the Holy Scriptures. (*My Life Today*, p. 176)

The Bible gives the true seeker an advanced mental drill; he comes from the contemplation of divine things with his faculties enriched. (*Lift Him Up*, p. 120)

Chapter Two
The Geometry of Power

Great is our Lord, and mighty in power;
His understanding is infinite. (Psalm 147:5)

I used to be pretty sharp at it—at geometry, that is—the branch of mathematics that deals with points, lines, shapes, and space. Yet, I've found that the old saying still rings true, "If you don't use it, you'll lose it," and I have lost most of my mathematic prowess, except for one law of geometry: If A=B, and B=C, then A=C. This transitive law has worked well for me in uncovering a definition for "grace" that can revolutionize the experience of anyone who makes the decision to practice using the information found in God's Word as the operational fuel for faith and choice. Notice what the word of God is called in this enlightening verse:

"So now, brethren, I commend you to God and to the word of His grace, which is able to build you up and give you an inheritance among all those who are sanctified." (Acts 20:32)

This verse tells us that we access God's upbuilding grace through His word! But what exactly is "grace"? Many people have been taught that God's grace is His unmerited favor that He extends to unworthy sinners who need saving from sin (Romans 3:23; Matthew 1:21). I would heartily agree! Our life-saving rescue from sin is made possible through Christ's sacrificial life and death (1 Peter 3:18). Again, I would heartily agree, for Ephesians 2:8, 9 paints a picture of this spiritual reality: *"For **by grace you have been saved through faith,** and that not of yourselves; it is the gift of God, not of works, lest anyone should boast."*

God's amazing grace is more than just unmerited favor.

However, God's amazing grace is more than just unmerited favor. And here's where geometry—spiritual geometry—comes into play to reveal another definition for this wonderful gift. We read in **Romans 1:16:**

*For I am not ashamed of **the gospel of Christ**, for **it is the power of God** to salvation for everyone who believes, for the Jew first and also for the Greek.*

Awesome! **The gospel of Christ is the power of God to save** everyone who believes, regardless of their ethnic background! But what does this powerful fact have to do with grace? Paul answers the question in **Acts 20:24:**

*But none of these things move me; nor do I count my life dear to myself, so that I may finish my race with joy, and the ministry which I received from the Lord Jesus, to testify to **the gospel of the grace of God**.*

Do you see what I emphasized? What is the gospel labeled here? It is *"the gospel of the grace of God"!*

So here's a little spiritual geometry—the geometry of spiritual power: If **(A) God's power to save** believers (Romans 1:16) is **the gospel (B)**, and if **the gospel (B)** is **(C) the grace of God** (Acts 20:24), then does it not make sense that God's grace must be His power to save believers? Yes, it does!

Here again is the geometrical formula, "If A = B, and B = C, then A = C," as applied in defining God's grace according to God's Word. So, if **A** (God's power to save believers) = **B** (the gospel, Romans 1:16), and **B** (the gospel) = **C** (God's grace, Acts 20:24), then **A** (God's power to save those who believe in Jesus) = **C** (God's grace)! Thus, God's grace is His power to save believers!

We see the power of grace exhibited in **Acts 4:33**, *"And with **great power** the apostles gave witness to the resurrection of the Lord Jesus. And **great grace** was upon them all."*

How do you suppose we are to access the powerful saving grace of God that heals broken hearts? **2 Peter 1:2–4** answers:

> ***Grace and peace be multiplied to you in the knowledge of God and of Jesus our Lord, as***

*His divine power has given to us all things that pertain to life and godliness, **through the knowledge of Him** who called us by glory and virtue, by which have been given to us **exceedingly great and precious promises**, that through these you may be partakers of the divine nature, having escaped the corruption that is in the world through lust.*

There you have it: The knowledge of God and His Son Jesus Christ as found in God's Word, which is *the word of His grace*, is the means by which Christ infuses His healing, favor-filled, power-packed grace into the hearts of those who make the decision to place their faith in Him.

It is through God's grace that He forgives us for our sins of the past. Such forgiveness is indeed His unmerited favor. But how wonderful it is to accept the reality that the Lord's amazing grace also empowers us to experience mental and emotional healing and to glorify Him in the way that we live! Such healing comes through His unlimited power! And guess how much of the Lord's empowering grace is available to you and me. Consider the following promise:

*And God is able to make **all grace** abound toward you, that you, **always** having **all** sufficiency in **all things**, may have an abundance for **every** good work. (2 Corinthians 9:8)*

Through this unfathomable gift, every circumstance of life that we face—no matter how challenging—can be a steppingstone to greater peace and joy as God's eternal plan of restoration comes to fruition in our lives.

I am so thankful for the provisions for healing and victory that our loving Creator and Re-creator has made available to us through His amazing grace! How about you? That's what this book is all about—understanding how to exercise the free gifts of faith and choice as fueled by the knowledge we gain from the Bible to remain on the receiving end of the eternally healing and saving power of God's grace.

Through this unfathomable gift, every circumstance of life that we face—no matter how challenging—can be a steppingstone to greater peace and joy as God's eternal plan of restoration comes to fruition in our lives.

Further Inspired Insight

Christ says: "Without Me ye can do nothing." Divine grace is the great element of saving power; without it all human efforts are unavailing. *(Testimonies for the Church, vol. 5, p. 583)*

The only remedy for the sins and sorrows of men is Christ. The gospel of His grace alone can cure the evils that curse society. *(Christ's Object Lessons, p. 254)*

The perfection of Christian character depends wholly upon the grace and strength found alone in God. *(Testimonies for the Church, vol. 3, p. 188)*

Chapter Three

The Healing Rescuer

*But without faith **it is** impossible to please Him, for he who comes to God must believe that He is, and that He is a rewarder of those who diligently seek Him. (Hebrews 11:6)*

Then He touched their eyes, saying, "According to your faith let it be to you." (Matthew 9:29)

"This is the work of God, that you believe in Him whom He sent." (John 6:29)

In **Hebrews 10:38, 39** is a thought-provoking statement: *"Now the just shall live by faith; but if anyone draws back, My soul has no pleasure in him. But we are not of those who draw back to perdition, but of those who* *believe to the saving of the soul."* I don't know about you, but the idea of drawing back to perdition with its eternal, dead-end future does not sound like a good outcome to me. Let's discover what saving faith—truly *believing to the saving of the soul*—looks like in real life. To do so, we need to understand what believing in God actually includes.

Mark chapter 9 begins our journey. A man brings his demon-possessed son to Christ's disciples to have the demon cast out. However, the disciples are unable to do so. When Jesus enters the scene, the man turns to Him and says, *"If You can do anything, have compassion on us and help us."* Jesus quietly replies, *"If you can believe, all things are possible to him that believes"* (Mark 9:22, 23). Wow! Such big words! All things are possible to him that believes? Right away the father cries out, *"I believe; help thou mine unbelief"* (Mark 9:24, KJV).

Perhaps in your personal experience you have cried out to God in the same way: *"I believe; help thou mine unbelief."* I sure have. Aren't you glad Jesus didn't walk away when the man cried, *"Help thou mine unbelief"*? If we truly desire His help, Jesus won't leave us in our moments of unbelief. However, this does call an important point to our attention. Christ tells us, in Luke 6:45, that the words that we speak originate from the abundance of what is in our heart, in other words, from the information that we have consistently chosen to fuel our thoughts. (See Chapter 1.) That abundance of information is the treasure that has captivated our hearts (Matthew 6:21). I would imagine that this anxious father carried memories from other futile attempts he had made over the years. These memories affected his ability to fully trust that Jesus could do what He claimed. Have you ever felt the same way? I have. The thoughts go kind of like this: "Lord, with all the past experiences I've had in trying to trust You, I believe that You should be able to help me, but I'm not completely sure that You can do what you claim to be able to do. So, if you can, please help me!" And the good news is this: As feeble and helpless as we may feel, *with our consent and cooperation*, Jesus can and will help us—just like He helped that hurting father, and, most often, it will be *"exceedingly abundantly above all that we"* ask *or think* (Ephesians 3:20)!

Wait a minute, Dan. I caught that—what do you mean by *"with our consent and cooperation"*? Here's what I mean: Believing happens in our heart (Romans 10:10). Our words come from the abundance, or treasure, of what's in our heart (Luke 6:45). So, now notice a fascinating insight found in 2 Corinthians 4:13: *"And since we have the same spirit of faith, according to what is written, 'I BELIEVED AND THEREFORE I SPOKE,' we also believe and therefore speak."* Do you see it? Where do the words that make up a person's speech come from? They come from what they believe in their heart! This is no coincidence! The information that we treasure in our heart is the fuel that feeds our thoughts, which produce our words. *That treasured information taken in determines our beliefs!* It's a wonderful thing when people decide to become sentinels over the information they feed their minds through their senses!

The truth of the matter is this:
With our power of choice, we decide
what type of information we are going
to place our faith in to
fuel our thoughts.

The truth of the matter is this: With our power of choice, we decide what type of information we are going to place our faith in to fuel our thoughts. We choose what type of information to feed our minds on. Then, as we consistently utilize that information in our thinking, it becomes the foundational authority for what we believe! The content of what we enjoy talking about is a direct result of what we believe to be valuable to our lives. Amazing! Information fuels our thoughts, and our thoughts produce our words—*and beliefs!*

Saving belief in God, then, entails a *faith decision* to not only trust the principles in God's Word as His truth for appraising the circumstances we face, but also—and get this—to exercise ongoing faith to order our thinking and responses according to the Bible's healing principles of truth! So, if a person desires to *believe to the saving of his soul*, what kind of information will he choose to trust and treasure in his heart? That's right—the truths of God found in the Bible, God's Word! What kind of information will such a person utilize to order his thoughts? God's truth about his circumstances! And here's where the rubber meets the road. If I am truly choosing to trust what God's Word tells me about the circumstances I am facing, what should I be training my mind to think? You've got it! I should be training my mind to think in harmony with the healing principles of God's Word concerning the circumstances I am facing! In reality, to *"believe to the saving of the soul,"* which is "salvation faith," is a heart-surrendered faith decision on our part, through the empowering grace of God (2 Corinthians 9:8), to trust and think only what God says in His Word to be the truth about any and every situation we face, every time it crops up in our thoughts. A person wanting to experience saving belief must, through grace-empowered faith, decide to wrap his thoughts around what the Lord says in His Word to be true about the situation that's vying for his mental attention, spiritual consideration, and physical response. And every time a questioning doubt arises concerning the situation, saving belief moves us, through the empowering grace of God, to cling to Christ through prayer **and to fasten our thoughts upon the truth** the Lord says, in His Word, we should think about that temptation. This is one of the most important reasons for habitually memorizing Bible texts, though not just any verse but verses that address specific circumstances that are tempting to us! Here's what God says about the Bible, His word:

The entirety of Your word is truth, and every one of Your righteous judgments endures forever. (Psalm 119:160)

"Believing to the saving of the soul"—this is the habit that, through grace-empowered faith, every sincere believer, in his life journey, must develop to promote godly mental

and spiritual health. True *saving belief* consists of a continuing grace-empowered faith decision (1) to trust what the Lord says in His word to be true about any circumstance we face and (2) to think only that which God has shown us from His Word should be the content of our thoughts about the situation we are facing. As a result, we will (3) respond to our circumstances in a way that will glorify the Lord (1 Corinthians 10:31).

"Believing to the saving of the soul"— this is the habit that, through grace-empowered faith, every sincere believer, in his life journey, must develop to promote godly mental and spiritual health.

Well, there's one additional element for healing spiritual victory that I believe is a vital component of saving belief. Along with trusting what God says to be true about our circumstances, fastening our thoughts upon that truth, and responding to glorify Him, is the blessing of (4) conversing with

God in prayer about the very truth that He has shown us in His Word must occupy our thoughts about our circumstances (Isaiah 26:3; Romans 12:12; 1 Thessalonians 5:17). *"Believing to the saving of the soul"* also includes the faith-engendered, grace-empowered, practice of immediately turning the attention of our thoughts to conversing with God in prayer about His thoughts of truth in His Word concerning the matter that tempts us every time it crops up for our attention until it becomes the habitual instant response of the heart, without having to think any other way about it ever! Let me illustrate this process for you. If someone says something bad about me and hurts my feelings, I will be tempted to think bad thoughts about that person and will in some way keep ruminating in my mind over what the person said, over what I can do to save face, or perhaps even over what I can do to get back at the person.

However, I truly want to experience salvation faith—*"believing to the saving of the soul"*—and I truly want real peace from God. So, by a faith-filled, grace-empowered choice to trust what the Lord says in His Word is true about me and about my offender, I immediately turn to God in my thoughts and determinedly converse with Him in prayer, thanking Him for what He thinks of me and my offender—the truth about us both found in His Word (Jeremiah 31:3; Romans 8:31, 38, 39; Ephesians 4:29–32; Philippians 4:6, 7; 1 Thessalonians 5:18).

Verses That Reveal How God Sees Things

For I know the thoughts that I think toward you, says the Lord, thoughts of peace and not of evil, to give you a future and a hope. (Jeremiah 29:11)

The Lord has appeared of old to me, saying: "Yes, I have loved you with an everlasting love; therefore with loving-kindness I have drawn you. (Jeremiah 31:3)

What then shall we say to these things? If God is for us, who can be against us? (Romans 8:31)

For I am persuaded that neither death nor life, nor angels nor principalities nor powers, nor things present nor things to come, nor height nor depth, nor any other created thing, shall be able to separate us from the love of God which is in Christ Jesus our Lord. (Romans 8:38, 39)

Let no corrupt word proceed out of your mouth, but what is good for necessary edification, that it may impart grace to the hearers. And do not grieve the Holy Spirit of God, by whom you were sealed for the day of redemption. Let all bitterness, wrath, anger, clamor, and evil speaking be put away from you, with all malice. And be kind to one another, tenderhearted, forgiving one another, even as God in Christ forgave you. (Ephesians 4:29–32)

Be anxious for nothing, but in everything by prayer and supplication, with thanksgiving, let your requests be made known to God; and the peace of God, which surpasses all understanding, will guard your hearts and minds through Christ Jesus. (Philippians 4:6, 7)

I can do all things through Christ who strengthens me. (Philippians 4:13)

In everything give thanks; for this is the will of God in Christ Jesus for you. (1 Thessalonians 5:18)

*"Blessed are you when men hate you,
And when they exclude you,
And revile you, and cast out your name as evil,
For the Son of Man's sake.
Rejoice in that day and leap for joy!*

For indeed your reward is great in heaven,
For in like manner their fathers did to the prophets." (Luke 6:22, 23)

By faith he forsook Egypt, not fearing the wrath of the king; for he endured as seeing Him who is invisible. (Hebrews 11:27)

My conversation with God might go something like this:

Lord, how can I thank You enough for what You've done through your selfless life and sacrificial death for me and _____ (the person who hurt me)! I am so grateful that You lived and died for me! It brings such peace to know that Your thoughts toward me and _____ are only thoughts of peace and not of evil (Jeremiah 29:11) and that You love me with an everlasting love (Jeremiah 31:3)! Thank you! It's such a blessing to know that you have told me that through You I can do everything you've asked of me (Philippians 4:13). Thank you for blessing me with the opportunity to forgive _____ the same way that You have forgiven me (Ephesians 4:32). I am so grateful that You know by experience what I am going through and that You endured it victoriously! Thank you for freeing me, not only to endure, but to rejoice regardless of what I'm feeling (Philippians 4:4). As you did with Moses, empower me to fasten my thoughts upon You, as seeing the invisible (Luke 6:22, 23; Hebrews 12:2, 3; 11:27).

Let me say it again—every time an unhealthy thought or feeling about what a person who has hurt me has said or done to me pops up in my thoughts, by grace-empowered faith I must immediately flee to God by directing my attention to conversing with Him about His thoughts toward me and my offender. As I continue to diligently follow this approach in dealing with the unhealthy thoughts and feelings surrounding an incident, what am I developing? I am developing a healing godly habit, and I am doing something else. I am learning to use these moments of temptation as catalysts for prompting me to flee to God in my thoughts, and I am giving all my attention to visiting with Him about what He thinks of me, my situation, and my offender.

There is more good news! Once this godly habit has been developed through practice to the point of its becoming the only way I think about any hurtful situation, **that truth-filled habit of thought will become my belief about that type of situation!** And what joy it is to realize that, when it has become the habit of my heart to converse with God in prayer about the truths of His word, the power of our archenemy to hold me captive has been broken! This is what *believing to the saving of the soul* is—true salvation faith! And what effect will this godly, faith-engendered, grace-empowered practice have upon my words and actions? Ah, you've got it—it will produce grace-empowered, faith-engendered, Spirit-inspired, Christ-like responses! (See 1 John 2:5, 6; 3:2, 3; 1 Peter 1:22, 23.)

Here it is again: The belief that ultimately will solidify my assurance that Jesus can and will save me is the habit of trusting God, of habitually placing my faith in Him in every situation I face. This means that by grace-empowered faith I am choosing to apply what the Lord says in His word to be the principles of truth and healthy response to every situation I face.

> *The belief that ultimately will solidify my assurance that Jesus can and will save me is the habit of trusting God, of habitually placing my faith in Him in every situation I face.*

How? Through the grace-empowered, faith-filled choice to continue to practice thinking thoughts that are in harmony with those healing and victorious principles, in thankful conversation with Him in prayer about His precious healing word. The fruit of such a determined, faith-inspired, grace-empowered mental and spiritual practice? Moved by love for Christ and Spirit-inspired desire to please Him, to the best of my knowledge and strength, I will respond in attitude, word, and action to honor Him and His eternally healing ways. 2 Corinthians 5:14–19. Be aware—this victorious heart-transforming combination of trusting God, thinking God's thoughts, and, in the privacy of my thoughts, giving my full attention to visiting with Him in prayer about what His Word says is the truth about my situation takes diligent faith-engendered, grace-empowered practice! But, recognizing that I am actually being empowered by the grace of God and cooperating with the Holy Spirit's working to develop true saving belief, which is *believing to the saving of my soul*, along with gaining victory over the enemy's tempting attacks, makes it eternally worth the grace-empowered, faith-filled effort! (See 1 Corinthians 15:10; 2 Corinthians 9:8; John 16:13.)

This practice is what Jesus modeled for us while He was here on earth! (See Philippians 2:5; Hebrews 2:13; 1 John 2:6.) Consider His experience in the wilderness of temptation. For every tempting idea that the devil threw at Him, a protective counter statement came out of His mouth. Read Matthew 4:3–11 and then answer the following questions: What information was Christ using in every counter statement He made? It was the truth of God's Word—a Bible statement that specifically negated the tempting idea the devil threw at Him! Why did God's Word come out of Christ's mouth? It was because it was hidden in the heart of His mind! (See Psalm 119:11.) Wow! And guess who was actually making the devil flee as Christ submitted His mind to think the truth? It was God the Father! (See Psalm 60:12; James 4:7.)

Christ's experience highlights the importance of Scripture memorization in the operation of saving belief. By memorizing Bible verses that contain God's truth concerning circumstances in our lives, which have tempted us to step outside of the Lord's will, we are actually training our minds in a vital component of saving belief, that is, in thinking Christ's thoughts about our circumstances!

Couple that training with a deepening love relationship with Jesus, which builds our trust in Him and the truthfulness of His healing ways and which directs our heart to find delight in constant communion with Him in prayer, and we have a winning combination—true *believing to the saving of the soul!* (See 2 Corinthians 5:14, 15; Philippians 2:5; Hebrews 10:39.)

Couple that training with a deepening love relationship with Jesus, which builds our trust in Him and the truthfulness of His healing ways and which directs our heart to find delight in constant communion with Him in prayer, and we have a winning combination—true believing to the saving of the soul!

Further Inspired Insight

By persistently reiterating falsehood, and that against all evidence, they at last come to believe it to be truth. (*Patriarchs and Prophets*, p. 403)

One accustoms himself to assert certain things in regard to himself, and at last he comes to believe them. Our thoughts produce our words and our words react upon our thoughts. (*That I May Know Him*, p. 137)

Our part is to rest on the Word with unwavering faith, believing that God will do according to His promise. Let faith cut its way through the shadow of the enemy. When a questioning doubt arises, go to Christ, and let the soul be encouraged by communion with Him. (*Signs of the Times*, September 26, 1900)

Converse with God through the medium of His Word. Thus our characters will be transformed. (*Sermons and Talks*, vol. 1, p. 286)

When Satan comes in, flooding the soul with his temptations, as he surely will, we may meet him with, "It is written." We may be shut in by the promises of God, which will be as a wall of fire about us. (*Signs of the Times*, May 22, 1884)

Chapter Four

"The Rescuer's Best Friend!"

Testifying to Jews, and also to Greeks, repentance toward God and faith toward our Lord Jesus Christ. (Acts 20:21)

In my personal journey of learning and practicing saving belief in Christ, one of the things I have become strongly convinced of is that I have done enough spiritual belly flopping to suffice for a lifetime! And I'm not done yet!

Regarding spiritual belly flops, I have the good intentions of obeying Christ as I dive into a pool of circumstances, only to end up "belly flopping"—landing flat on my spiritual belly and face as I respond out of my old unhealthy habit of protecting self and dishonoring my Lord. You too? And, then, to top it off, I don't just fall once, but I fall numerous times under similar circumstances! Do you know what I mean? For the hundredth time, you catch yourself falling into some bad habit that's plagued you for years. You've sincerely and repeatedly asked God to forgive you and give you victory. And, with the failure, come strong feelings of guilt and condemnation because the person you trusted to tell you the truth said, "If you have really repented, you wouldn't do it again!" That idea is stuck in your thoughts, and then some semblance of this kind of thought slips into your awareness: "You're never going to conquer this—it's too strong—you've been doing it for too long!"

Are you screaming "help"
by now, as I have done
so many times?

Are you screaming "help" by now, as I have done so many times? Well, there's good news—through saving belief and its best friend, it is possible to be freed from these disconcerting experiences and find the victorious healing that Jesus lived and died to provide us!

Consider with me these hope-filled words of our Lord found in **Hebrews 12:1, 2**:

Therefore we also, since we are surrounded by so great a cloud of witnesses, let us lay aside every weight, and the sin which so easily ensnares us, and let us run with endurance the race that is set before us, looking unto Jesus, the author and finisher of our faith, who for the joy that was set before Him endured the cross, despising the shame, and has sat down at the right hand of the throne of God.

Do you see it? What is it possible for us to experience? *"Let us lay aside every weight, and the sin which so easily ensnares us."* Really? *Hmmm*—I think it might be time to begin practicing saving belief, what do you say?

What does *"looking unto Jesus"* have to do with laying aside *"every weight and sin which so easily ensnares us"*? Let's answer that question by introducing the very best friend of *saving belief.* Notice what Jesus shared in His version of preaching the gospel of the kingdom of God, as found in Mark 1:15:

> *"The time is fulfilled, and the kingdom of God is at hand. Repent, and believe in the gospel."*

Do you see it? What accompanies believing? *Repentance*—and Acts 5:31 calls it a gift! Also, according to Jesus, *repentance* is a major player that works together with *saving belief* to accomplish the victory and to bring the healing offered through the gospel! But the repentance that Christ offers as a gift is not repentance as most people understand the term. Along with saving belief, when *true repentance* is understood and exercised the way that God intended, it brings victory and healing over "every weight, and the sin which so easily ensnares us"! Follow along as we meet the best friend of saving belief.

First of all, notice in 2 Corinthians 7:9–11 the compelling mindset in true healing repentance:

Now I rejoice, not that you were made sorry, but that your sorrow led to repentance. For you were made sorry in a godly manner, that you might suffer loss from us in nothing. For godly sorrow produces repentance leading to salvation, not to be regretted; but the sorrow of the world produces death. For observe this very thing, that you sorrowed in a godly manner: What diligence it produced in you, what clearing of yourselves, what indignation, what fear, what vehement desire, what zeal, what vindication! In all things you proved yourselves to be clear in this matter.

Wow! There are at least two important realities about the repentance spoken of here: (1) A sorrowful feeling is not conclusive evidence of repentance that leads to salvation. If it is worldly sorrow, it leads to death (v. 10). Godly sorrow works a change of heart that doesn't need repentance. (2)

To understand the mindset of godly repentance, contemplate the words describing repentance that comes from godly sorrow: "diligence," "clearing of yourselves," "indignation," "fear," "vehement desire," "zeal," and "vindication." What would you say those words indicate about godly repentance? May I suggest that they reveal that, in true godly repentance, there is not an iota of desire in a person's heart to repeat or continue the sinful activity! Why? Because the Holy Spirit has worked a renovating miracle of divine grace in the heart! It is His gift alone because only He can change a person's heart!

But there's more to the gift than just this miracle! Contrary to what many believe, repentance *is not a one-time event* of quitting an unhealthy activity, *never to do it again* because we've lost all desire to do so! Have I got your attention? Rather, true godly repentance that must accompany saving belief produces a radical God-given, grace-empowered heart change *in a person's thinking* that stimulates *an ongoing, grace-empowered, practice* of responding to circumstances in ways that glorify the Lord and His loving character (Acts 5:31; 1 Corinthians 10:31). You may have guessed already, but we have partially hit on this aspect of true repentance in the last chapter. The Greek root word from which "repentance" is translated simply means "to think differently." When people decide by faith to think only God's thoughts *instead of their own* about the tempting or trying circumstance confronting them, they are experiencing, through the empowering work of the Holy Spirit, a vital aspect of the Lord's gift of repentance!

Now, let's add some frosting to the cake of godly repentance! Here's another extremely important aspect of the Lord's gift of godly repentance: in the original Greek text, when the verb "repent" in Mark 1:15 is parsed (that is, grammatically analyzed), it actually is speaking of an ongoing action—an ongoing practice—not a one-time event! Why is this aspect of repentance so important? Because most of the damaging thoughts, feelings, and actions we carry are well-developed habits! And you don't just quit an automatic response to a threatening trigger, that is, a circumstance that stimulates a person to react out of habit! It takes repeated, grace-empowered, faith-engendered practice!

So, please remember this: Deliverance from any damaging habit is an ongoing battle, not a one-time event! Take it from me—one of the most challenging but awesome Spirit-inspired, grace-empowered experiences, yielding wonderfully healing results in your life, is the grace-empowered, faith-engendered practice of godly repentance and saving belief. These take place when you, through Spirit-inspired, faith-engendered, grace-empowered practice, determinedly think Christ's thoughts about every tempting circumstance that pops up in your life and bring every thought captive to the obedience of Christ, an obedience He modeled for us when the devil tempted Him.

How often do you need to practice thinking Christ's thoughts? Over and over and over again—every time a temptation tries to capture your thoughts—practice keeping your mind upon the Lord, thinking only His thoughts of truth about that temptation, conversing with Him in thankful prayer until this saving response becomes a habitual part of your life, kicking in automatically in the face of every temptation! I can tell you from my Christian practice—as challenging as true godly repentance sounds—it works! Why? Because it is a faith-engendered, grace-empowered gift from God! (See Acts 5:31; 2 Corinthians 9:8; 1 John 5:4.) This, I believe, is what Isaiah 26:3 means when it says: *"You will keep him in perfect peace, Whose mind is stayed on You, Because he trusts in You."*

And, count on it, if the heart is responding trustingly to the work of the Holy Spirit, it will stimulate a person not only to victorious repentance and saving belief but also to spiritual fruit-filled physical action!

And, count on it, if the heart is responding trustingly to the work of the Holy Spirit, it will stimulate a person not only to victorious repentance and saving belief but also to spiritual fruit-filled physical action! (See Ezekiel 36:26, 27; Philippians 2:12, 13.)

Further Inspired Insight

Repentance toward God and faith in Jesus Christ are the fruits of the renewing power of the grace of the Spirit. **Repentance represents the process** by which the soul seeks to reflect the image of Christ to the world. (*My Life Today*, p. 49)

Repentance for sin is the first fruits of the working of the Holy Spirit in the life. **It is the only process** by which infinite purity reflects the image of Christ in His redeemed subjects. (*Seventh-day Adventist Bible Commentary*, volume 6, p. 1068)

The life we live is to be one of **continual repentance** and humility. **We need to repent constantly,** that we may be constantly victorious. When we have true humility, we have victory. The enemy never can take out of the hand of Christ the one who is simply trusting in His promises. (*Seventh-day Adventist Bible Commentary*, vol. 7, p. 959)

If he [David] **had but removed his mind from the distressing situation in which he was placed, and had thought of God's power and majesty,** he would have been at peace even in the midst of the shadows of death ... (*Patriarchs and Prophets*, p. 657)

Chapter Five

Capturing Emotional Bandits

For though we walk in the flesh, we do not war according to the flesh. For the weapons of our warfare are not carnal but mighty in God for pulling down strongholds, casting down arguments and every high thing that exalts itself against the knowledge of God, bringing every thought into captivity to the obedience of Christ. (2 Corinthians 10:3–5)

The first Easter Sunday of history was over. The two disciples who met Christ on their way to Emmaus had rushed back to Jerusalem to share the earth-shaking news that their Master and Friend had risen from the dead! He was alive! We take up the story in Luke 24:36:

Now as they said these things, Jesus Himself stood in the midst of them, and said to them, "Peace to you." But they were terrified and frightened, and supposed they had seen a spirit. And He said to them, "Why are you troubled? And why do doubts arise in your hearts?"

It has happened to me; it has probably happened to you. No, I'm not talking about Christ suddenly appearing at your Monday morning conference. I'm talking about an event that takes you by surprise. For example, you step into your backyard to enjoy your newly planted flower patch, and, instead of a colorful array of happy flowers, you find that the neighbor's dog has dug up a major portion of your hard work to bury his leftovers! Let me ask you, besides unkind thoughts about the dog (and possibly his owner), what else do you experience? Answer: You experience what the disciples experienced when Jesus suddenly appeared in their midst—strong emotions! That's not unusual. It happens all the time in people's lives. But back to the disciples—here's an important question: When Christ suddenly appeared in their midst, why did they initially experience fright and terror rather than joy over the Savior's resurrection? Did you see the answer in verse 37? It was what they were thinking! They supposed that they had seen a spirit, which is to say, a ghost! And it brought emotional turmoil. It brought feelings of fear and unrest! That's why Jesus asked those questions in verse 38—*"Why are you troubled? And why do doubts arise in your hearts?"*

You step into your backyard to enjoy your newly planted flower patch, and, instead of a colorful array of happy flowers, you find that the neighbor's dog has dug up a major portion of your hard work to bury his leftovers!

Now notice what begins to happen to the disciples' emotions as Jesus gives them physical evidence of His presence and as it begins to dawn upon them that this really is their risen Savior and Friend:

*"Behold My hands and My feet, that it is I Myself. Handle Me and see, for a spirit does not have flesh and bones as you see I have." When He had said this, He showed them His hands and His feet. But while they still did not believe **for joy, and marveled**, He said to them, "Have you any food here?" So they gave Him a piece of a broiled fish and some honeycomb. And He took it and ate in their presence. (Luke 24:39–43)*

Awesome! They went from terror and fright to marveling joy through a metamorphosis of their thoughts about Christ! This is an extremely valuable insight for anyone who desires to experience emotional healing. The catalyst for the feelings we have about our life circumstances is most often instigated and intensified by what we are thinking about the situation we are facing. This is vital to understand. Any way our enemy, the devil and his angels, can get a person to begin and continue to dwell in his thoughts on false information about God, about himself, about other people, or about his circumstances, he is gaining a foothold of control, not only upon their physical lives but also upon their emotions!

They went from terror and fright to marveling joy through a metamorphosis of their thoughts about Christ!

Oh how grateful we can be for God's truth and gracious empowerment to enable us to *"believe to the saving of the soul"* (Hebrews 10:39)—through grace-empowered faith—to bring the thoughts of our heart into captivity to Christ and dwell upon the truth from His Word in thankful prayer about every situation we face when it pops into mind! (See 2 Corinthians 10:3–5.) This is how we can capture the emotional bandits that rob us of energy, hope, and life! This is how Jesus thrived under the relentless temptations of the enemy. It's the only way that you and I can survive and thrive as we are surrounded by the temptations of our day. The prayer-filled, faith-engendered, grace-empowered practice of saving belief and godly repentance produces healthy emotions! Truthfully, you do not have to remain trapped in a whirlpool of damaging emotions! You can put those bandits in jail—without parole!

Further Inspired Insight

Faith is not a happy flight of feeling; it is simply taking God at His word—believing that He will fulfill His promises because He said He would. Hope in God, trust in Him, and rest in His promises, whether you feel happy or not. A good emotion is no evidence that you are a child of God, neither are disturbed, troubled, perplexing feelings an evidence that you are not a child of God. Come to the Scriptures and intelligently take God at His word. Comply with the conditions and believe He will accept you as His child. Be not faithless, but believing. (*Our High Calling*, p. 119)

The religion of Christ is not a religion of mere emotion. You cannot depend upon your feelings for an evidence of acceptance with God, for feelings are variable. You must plant your feet on the promises of God's Word ... and learn to live by faith ... Now, the feelings must not be made the test of the spiritual state, be they good or be they discouraging. The word of God is to be our evidence of our true standing before Him. Many are bewildered on this point ... (*In Heavenly Places*, p. 126)

The feelings, whether encouraging or discouraging, should not be made the test of the spiritual condition. By God's Word we are to determine our true standing before Him. Many are bewildered on this point. When they are happy and joyous, they think that they are accepted of God. When a change comes, and they feel depressed, they think that God has forsaken them ... God does not desire us to go through life with a distrust of Him ... While we were yet sinners, God gave

His Son to die for us. Can we doubt His goodness? ... (*In Heavenly Places*, p. 131)

By steadfastly keeping the will on the Lord's side, every emotion will be brought into captivity to the will of Jesus. You will then find your feet on solid rock. It will take, at times, every particle of will power which you possess; but it is God that is working for you, and you will come forth from the molding process a vessel unto honor. (*Testimonies for the Church*, vol. 5, p. 514)

Chapter Six

Victory's Indomitable Motivator

*Now hope does not disappoint, because the
love of God has been poured out in
our hearts by the Holy Spirit who
was given to us. (Romans 5:5)*

God's healing Word, saving belief
empowered by grace, godly repentance,
and earnest conversation with God through
continuous prayer are awesome gifts when
utilized through grace-empowered, faith-
engendered practice under the circumstances
that God allows to knock on your door. But
what keeps you practicing these gifts when
they don't seem to be working as you pictured

or when things appear to be going the wrong way or when it seems that you are losing instead of gaining or when people make fun of your sincere desire and activity to better your life? These are important considerations. The Bible gives us a reality check.

It was a seemingly invincible Peter who responded to Christ's statement in Matthew 26:31 that all of His disciples would be offended the night of His betrayal and arrest in Gethsemane. Consider Peter's response: *"Peter answered and said to Him, 'Even if all are made to stumble because of You, I will never be made to stumble' "* (Matthew 26:33). So, what really happened? Peter ended up denying his Lord three times after Christ was taken captive to be falsely tried and crucified (Matthew 26:69–75). And then there was Simon the sorcerer, who believed and was baptized through Philip's preaching of Christ. Simon saw the miracles being done by the apostles, and, when he witnessed believers receiving the Holy Spirit as hands were laid on them, he offered the apostles money to get the same power for himself (Acts 8:17–19).

What would be the motivation behind Peter's denial of the Savior after walking with Him for three and a half years? What would be the motivation behind Simon's offering money to get something that God freely bestows? The Bible gives only one valid reason for such actions. 2 Timothy 3:2 says, *"men shall be lovers of their own selves ..."* Contrary to contemporary Christian ideas, "love for self" is a hindrance—not a solution—to the majority of mental and spiritual maladies. Love of self was revealed in Peter's denial of Christ to avoid pain and discomfort. It was witnessed in Simon's desire to gain something he wanted.

So, what did Jesus mean in Matthew 22:39 when He said, *"You shall love your neighbor as yourself?"* The little two-letter word "as" in that verse gives us an important insight. It is translated from the Greek word that is used throughout the New Testament as a word of *comparison,* not as a word of *command.* So, Jesus was actually giving the lawyer who was trying to trap Him—and us—a comparison that we, in our fallen condition, could understand. He was saying to love others as much as we love ourselves! Yet, as we just discovered, love for self is still a problem and not a solution! So, in reality, how does Jesus actually want His followers to love their fellowman? Before He was crucified, Christ gave a command to his disciples that gives us His directive for our relationships with others and clarifies what He meant when He said, *"Love your neighbor as yourself"* (Mark 12:31). *"A new commandment I give to you, that you love one another; as I have loved you, that you also love one another"* (John 13:34). *"This is My commandment, that you love one another as I have loved you"* (John 15:12). Do you see it? Christ's directive is for us to love others the way He loved us!" 2 Corinthians 5:14, 15 reads:

> *For the love of Christ compels us, because we judge thus: that if One died for all, then all died; and He died for all, that those who live should live no longer for themselves, but for Him who died for them and rose again.*

Precious reader, love for Christ and His sacrificial love for us—the love that kept

Him faithful unto death—is the only motivation that will sustain us in this faith-engendered, grace-empowered healing practice of cooperating with God's Spirit to *believe to the saving of the soul.* To love our neighbor and love one another as Christ has loved us, and, yes, to respect and care for our body and mind as Christ's valuable temple (1 Corinthians 6:19, 20) are God's call for Christian believers! But here is reality: You and I cannot produce this kind of self-sacrificing love! (See Jeremiah 13:23.) Christ's love can only be received from Jesus Himself through the working of the Holy Spirit in our hearts! (See Romans 5:5; 2 Corinthians 5:14, 15.)

Here is reality: You and I cannot produce this kind of self-sacrificing love!

So, how then, does a person place himself or herself on the receiving end of the Holy Spirit's work to imbue his or her heart with this kind of love, which is a vital component of the life of victory? There is only one way:

Now the Lord is the Spirit; and where the Spirit of the Lord is, there is liberty. But we all, with unveiled face, beholding as in a mirror the glory of the Lord, are being transformed into the same image from glory to glory, just as by the Spirit of the Lord. (2 Corinthians 3:17, 18)

These verses make it clear that the Holy Spirit definitely wants to bring us liberty. Our part in His work is to *behold the glory of the Lord* with an unveiled heart that has turned to the Lord (vss. 15, 16). Besides His awesome majesty and splendor, God's glory represents His character! (See Exodus 33:18, 19; 34:5–7.) No man has seen God the Father (John 1:18), but Christ Jesus came to reveal the Father's character to us in His self-sacrificing life and death (John 14:9). If, in our desire to know God, we make a daily faith-engendered, grace-empowered decision to spend time earnestly contemplating and studying the life of Christ in the Gospels of Matthew, Mark, Luke, and John, then we put ourselves in a position with the Lord to be changed into His image by the work of the

Holy Spirit upon our hearts! In other words, through the work of the Holy Spirit, the Lord's character of love is being transferred to our lives! We are receiving more and more of His divine nature! (See 2 Peter 1:2–4; 1 John 4:8.) And here's some more good news: as more and more of Christ's character of love is transposed into our hearts (Romans 5:5), our self-centered motivation will begin to change. With a desire to practice trusting in Him with all our heart, choosing to think only His thoughts about our circumstances, engaging in thankful, intimate, and continual converse with Him in prayer, and glorifying Him in our daily activities, our desire and motivation for all these activities will only increase! Every other motivation will begin to lose its control over our thoughts, choices, and actions! Amen!

Further Inspired Insight

A thoroughgoing Christian draws his motives of action from his deep heart-love for his Master. Up through the roots of his affection for Christ springs an unselfish interest in his brethren. Love imparts to its possessor grace, propriety, and comeliness of deportment. It illuminates the countenance and subdues the voice; it refines and elevates the entire being. (*Gospel Workers*, p. 123)

When self is submerged in Christ, true love springs forth spontaneously. It is not an emotion or an impulse but a decision of a sanctified will. It consists not in feeling but in the transformation of the whole heart, soul, and character, which is dead to self and alive unto God. (*Mind, Character, and Personality*, vol. 1, p. 206)

Supreme love for God and unselfish love for one another—this is the best gift that our heavenly Father can bestow. This love is not an impulse, but a divine principle, a permanent power. The unconsecrated heart cannot originate or produce it. Only in the heart where Jesus reigns is it found. "We love Him, because He first loved us." [1 John 4:19.] In the heart renewed by divine grace, love is the ruling principle of action. (*The Acts of the Apostles*, p. 551)

The deep love of God alone will sustain the soul amid the trials which are just upon us. (*Testimonies for the Church*, vol. 5, p. 135)

Chapter Seven

The Faithful Workmen of Restoration

Being confident of this very thing, that He who has begun a good work in you will complete it until the day of Jesus Christ.
(Philippians 1:6)

Sometimes what we believe to be the worst news can turn out to be the best news. I think it's this way with God and whatever He allows us to experience to give us every possible opportunity to know His peace and healing through prayer-filled, faith-engendered, grace-empowered, godly repentance and saving belief. Is there a reason for this? Yes! He has an ultimate goal in His plans for us, something that encapsulates spiritual and emotional healing! What might that be? Let's wrestle with this text in God's Word and find the answer:

> *And we know that all things work together for good to those who love God, to those who are the called according to His purpose. For whom He foreknew, He also predestined to be conformed to the image of His Son, that He might be the firstborn among many brethren. (Romans 8:28, 29)*

Question: According to these two verses, for those who love Him, what is the end result of everything that the Lord God permits us to experience? Answer: It works together for good!

OK, in your opinion, to all outward appearances, has everything the Lord has permitted you to experience, turned out to be or even appeared to be "good?" No? Why not? Well, in my experience, I can truthfully say that sometimes I've been threatened by what the Lord allowed me to go through. When a TIA (transient ischemic attack) took away the mobility of a whole side of my body and stole my ability to talk, tempting thoughts started knocking on the door of my heart that the "*good* life" of ministry was over for me.

So why does God allow things like this to happen? What "good" can come out of the Lord allowing such circumstances to suddenly make their appearance in our lives? Do you see the answer in Romans 8:28, 29? According to these verses, what is the "good" that God promises will come out of the "all things" that He allows? Here's a clue: According to these verses, what are Christ's followers predestined to experience? To be *conformed to the image of His Son*! Yes! To be like Christ! Really? Yes, really! That was God's original plan! Mankind was originally created in His image (Genesis 1:26, 27). Sin damaged that image in all of us (Romans 3:23). But our loving Creator and Redeemer has provided a way for us to be restored back to the way He created us—to be like Him— to cooperate with His Holy Spirit to develop His victorious and healing character of love in real life! (See 2 Samuel 14:14.) And, most often He couples, with our daily time of beholding His loving gracious character (see chapter 5), restoration through the trials of circumstances, which threaten our sense of well-being and stimulate questioning doubts. For some reason, God knows that these trying experiences do something for our hearts that nothing else can. Perhaps the major reason why God allows trying situations in the landscape of our lives is communicated in Deuteronomy 8:2:

> *"And you shall remember that the LORD your God led you all the way these forty years in the wilderness, to humble you and test you, to know what was in your heart, whether you would keep His commandments or not."*

Did you notice the reason that God allows the wilderness tests of trial in the lives of those He loves? Does the phrase *"to know what was in your heart"* ring a bell? God already knows what hides in the habits of our hearts (Psalm 44:21; 139:1–4). But who doesn't know? We don't! We don't know what is in our hearts (Jeremiah 17:9). And a major trap that we fall into is trusting our own heart! (See Proverbs 28:26; 21:2; 16:25.) It seems, in our fallen condition, that the only way we can get a true picture of what is in our heart and is damaging our lives and jeopardizing our future is through the trials that God allows us to experience and—get this—not to hurt us but to do us "good in the end" (Deuteronomy 8:16), as we read in Romans 8:28! So, remember this: **Our responses** to the circumstances that bother us, worry us, make us angry, and stimulate anxiety and fear give us the opportunity to see what lies hidden and latent in ourselves and that is actually keeping us in bondage and damaging our lives! *As a man thinks in his heart, so is he* (Proverbs 23:7). **Our responses** reveal the habits of thought in our hearts that need to be surrendered and transformed through prayer-filled, true and godly repentance and saving belief! Does this fact make you angry or cause you to doubt whether God really has your best interest in mind? Hmmm. I wonder if the Lord could be giving you opportunities right now through grace-empowered faith to practice God-given repentance and saving belief?

If people sincerely love God and desire to be like Him and spend eternity with Him, it is possible for them, like the apostle Paul, to actually come to the point of seeing trials as something for which to be thankful!

The truth of the matter is this: If people sincerely love God and desire to be like Him and spend eternity with Him, it is possible for them, like the apostle Paul, to actually come to the point of seeing trials as something for which to be thankful! (See 2 Corinthians 12:9, 10; 1 Thessalonians 5:18.) Through the difficulties He allows us to face, our loving Lord gives us opportunities to recognize our weaknesses and to make, of our own volition, a faith-filled, grace-empowered decision to turn to Him for help and practice godly repentance and saving belief in our responses to trials! Amazingly, He does so without manipulating, coercing, or forcing our power of choice! For what purpose? Here it is again: *"To do you good in the end"* (Deuteronomy 8:16). And something else—as we, through grace-empowered, faith engendered, prayer-filled choices, practice responding through godly repentance and saving belief, we give others a picture of what God can do for hurting humans who accept Him as Lord and who practice His healing ways. He is being glorified! Amen!

So here it is again: As we encounter circumstances that bother us, worry us, make us sad, make us angry, or stimulate fear, we generally respond in the habitual ways that we have developed over time for handling such circumstances to protect ourselves from harm. However, if God knows that our habitual responses are ultimately damaging to us and keeping us from experiencing the true peace and healing His ways provide, how can He make us realize what is happening without manipulating, coercing, or forcing our power of choice?

You may know by now how I'm going to answer: He allows us to face circumstances that give us the opportunity to practice trusting Him and to respond to the circumstances in a way to glorify Him, not only in our actions but, more importantly, in the way we think about those challenging circumstances. By the faith practice of "believing to the saving of the soul," we are cooperating with the Holy Spirit to develop the very habit of trusting that the Lord desires the best for us in this life and in the life to come! In the process, we enjoy the privilege of witnessing to the transforming power of His infinite grace to a society of anxious and hurting people who engage in all kinds of activities in search of peace and true healing.

By the faith practice of "believing to the saving of the soul," we are cooperating with the Holy Spirit to develop the very habit of trusting that the Lord desires the best for us in this life and in the life to come!

Throughout this process, there are a few things that are important to keep in mind: (1) In most if not all cases of mental and spiritual dysfunction, healing involves replacing old unhealthy habits of thinking with new godly habits of thinking about the things that bother us, worry us, make us fearful, make us angry, and that encourage hopelessness and other negative feelings. As our habitual viewpoint of circumstances begins to improve, our feelings and willingness to respond healthfully will also progress in a godly direction. (2) Because old habits die hard, it requires prayer-filled, faith-engendered, grace-empowered perseverance and effort to retrain the mind to habitually think healthfully about the circumstances of life that have railroaded and derailed our hearts. Remember, repentance is an ongoing process—not a one-time event. (See Chapter 4.) (3) In this author's opinion, the only motivation strong enough to move anyone to persist in the work of dehabituation (putting off the old man) and rehabituation (putting on the new Christ-like man, Ephesians 4:22–24) is the love for Christ that Christ gives through His Holy Spirit.

Further Inspired Insight

The Father's presence encircled Christ, and nothing befell Him but that which infinite love permitted for the blessing of the world. Here was His source of comfort, and it is for us. He who is imbued with the Spirit of Christ abides in Christ. Whatever comes to him comes from the Saviour, who surrounds him with His presence. Nothing can touch him except by the Lord's permission. All our sufferings and sorrows, all our temptations and trials, all our sadness and griefs, all our persecutions and privations, in short, all things work together for our good. All experiences and circumstances are God's workmen whereby good is brought to us. (*The Ministry of Healing*, pp. 488, 489)

The children of God may rejoice in all things and at all times. When troubles and difficulties come, believing in the wise providences of God, you may rejoice. You need not wait for a happy flight of feeling, but by faith you may lay hold of the promises, and lift up a hymn of thanksgiving to God. When Satan tempts you, breathe not a word of doubt or darkness. You may have your choice as to who shall rule your heart and control your mind. (*Review and Herald*, February 11, 1890)

That which you look upon as disaster is the door to highest benefit. (*Thoughts from the Mount of Blessing*, p. 61)

Chapter Eight

Taking Advantage of God's Workmen

My brethren, count it all joy when you fall into various trials, knowing that the testing of your faith produces patience. But let patience have its perfect work, that you may be perfect and complete, lacking nothing. (James 1:2–4)

What? Taking advantage of trials? Yes, as I have considered what our loving Lord is telling us from His Word, that's the conclusion I've come to in my personal life. I encourage you to contemplate this sequence of Bible verses: **Jeremiah 29:11**—No matter what we face, God's thoughts toward you and me are "thoughts of peace and not of evil."

John 19:11—Nothing can touch us except by the Lord's permission. **Luke 10:19**—Christ promises that nothing He allows will by any means hurt us. **1 Corinthians 10:13**—When something Jesus allows threatens us, rattles our cage, or shakes our sense of well-being, He promises never to allow us to be tempted above what we are able but will always provide a way for us to remain faithful and obedient to Him through the trial. **Romans 8:28, 29** makes it clear that all things the Lord allows to take place will work together for our good that we may be conformed to His image. Therefore, according to **James 1:2–4**, we can *"count it all joy when you fall into various trials, knowing that the testing of your faith produces patience."* Why count it all joy when our faith is tested? Because of the perfect work faith-testing produces! *"But let patience have its perfect work, that you may be perfect and complete, lacking nothing."* Perfect and complete, lacking nothing—these are God's ultimate goal in giving us the opportunity to train under His care! Notice how Christ states this in these two translations of Luke 6:40:

*The disciple is not above his master: but every one **that is perfect** shall be as his master. (Luke 6:40, KJV)*

*"A disciple is not above his teacher, but everyone **who is perfectly trained** will be like his teacher." (Luke 6:40, NKJV)*

To be like Jesus—that's the call! If you and I are willing to be perfectly trained through prayer-filled, faith-engendered, grace-empowered cooperation with the Holy Spirit, the Lord who began a good work in us will carry it through to bring us complete recovery from the damage that sin has caused. Yes! This is true restoration to God's original design (Philippians 1:6; Genesis 1:26, 27).

This powerful work of transforming our lives to be like Jesus will continue until Christ comes to take His ransomed children home to heaven! (See Philippians 1:6.) Nothing short of continuous, spiritual growth through faith-filled, grace-empowered study and practice of God's Word can prepare a person to welcome Christ when He comes the second time.

*That is what this book is all about—
providing an understanding of the
spiritual mechanics involved in
cooperating with the Lord in His
wonderful work of preparing us to spend
eternity with Him!*

That is what this book is all about—
providing an understanding of the spiritual
mechanics involved in cooperating with the
Lord in His wonderful work of preparing us
to spend eternity with Him! (See John 14:1–
3; 1 John 3:2, 3.)

I believe this is why the Lord encourages
us to practice rejoicing in prayerful thankfulness at all times:

*Rejoice always, pray without ceasing, in
everything give thanks; for this is the will of
God in Christ Jesus for you.* (1 Thessalonians 5:16–18)

OK, so where does a person start in the
practice of taking advantage of trials? Here
are some pointers:

(1) Start with the circumstance that most recently has bothered you, worried you, made you fearful, or angry. Regardless of the type of emotions you may be experiencing, make a grace-empowered, faith-engendered decision to trust what the Lord instructs His people to do in 1 Thessalonians 5:18 and begin thanking Him for the circumstance and everyone involved without expecting any personal benefit—even though it may not be resolved yet, hasn't turned out the way you wanted, or hasn't stimulated any change in the attitude of the other people involved. That you are willing to take this action by grace-empowered faith and to thank God for the trial is evidence of the work of the Spirit of grace in your heart.

(2) With a humble willingness in your heart to practice saving belief, godly repentance, and thank-filled prayer, contemplate this question: What is it about this circumstance that bothers me? What is it that makes me feel the way I do about it? Is it what I or someone else did? Is it my atti-

tude or someone else's? Is it because of what happened to me or someone else? Is it the fact that I lost someone or something valuable to me? Is it because I don't know what to think about it, how to react to it, or how to handle the shame, pain, or embarrassment that it has produced?

(3) Then, in the light of your answer to #2, clinging to sincere honesty with God, ask yourself, what have I been thinking, and am I still thinking about the disquieting answer that the questions of #2 have revealed?

(4) Test your answer to #3 with the following question:

Have my past and present thoughts, disclosed by question #3, been pleasing to the Lord? Are they the kind of thoughts the Lord would have me think? If they are not biblical, godly thoughts or if you're not sure if your thoughts are acceptable to the Lord's healing ways, ask Him to show you from His Word what you should be thinking about the circumstance. Then, by grace-empowered faith, be willing to search God's Word for what He would have you to practice thinking (2 Corinthians 13:5; Psalm 139:23, 24; Jeremiah 29:13).

(5) When God does show you what He would have you think about an unsettling circumstance whenever it vies for your attention, by grace-empowered faith, diligently practice thinking only the Lord's thoughts concerning the trial with prayer-filled thankfulness and rejoicing in your heart, knowing that you are actually cooperating with the workings of God's Spirit to transform the heart of your mind (Romans 12:2).

(6) If, by earnestly searching the Word of God, you cannot immediately find the insights that clearly indicate what Jesus would want you to think about an unsettling circumstance, don't despair. Just take even the delay as an opportunity to practice trusting Him and thanking Him for the trial—even though He

hasn't shown you from His Word what to think. Your practice of thankfulness is an evidence of your trust! This too is training in waiting upon the Lord, which gives Him the right to strengthen your heart (Psalm 27:14). Continue to take time daily to diligently seek for additional wisdom and understanding concerning the trial.

If, by earnestly searching the Word of God, you cannot immediately find the insights that clearly indicate what Jesus would want you to think about an unsettling circumstance, don't despair.

Precious reader, you can be confident of this very thing, *that He who has begun a good work in you will complete it until the day of Jesus Christ!* (See Philippians 1:6 and Psalm 138:8.) Amen!

Further Inspired Insight

To wait patiently, to trust when everything looks dark, is the lesson that the leaders in God's work need to learn. Heaven will not fail them in their day of adversity. Nothing is apparently more helpless, yet really more invincible, than the soul that feels its nothingness, and relies wholly on God. (*Prophets and Kings*, pp. 174, 175)

God permitted your surroundings to exist to develop character. But you could have made your surroundings; for by resisting or enduring temptation, circumstances are controlled by the might of the will in the name of Jesus. This is overcoming as Christ overcame. "This is the victory that overcometh the world, even our faith." (*Testimonies for the Church*, vol. 4, p. 346)

Through affliction God reveals to us the plague spots in our characters, that by His grace we may overcome our faults. (*The Desire of Ages*, p. 301)

Chapter Nine

The Great Identity Exchange!

For this is the will of God, your sanctification:
... For God did not call us to uncleanness,
but in holiness. (1 Thessalonians 4:3, 7)

Christ identified Himself with us that we, in reality, might be enabled to identify with Him. We see this precious experience in the metamorphosis of a shaky young high school student into a Christ-like caring physician! Oh how wonderful it would be if, in this world, all identity exchanges were positive as this!

The truth of the matter is that stealing someone else's identity is big business in this world. However, there is one identity no other human being can steal from anyone else, and that is character identity—that is, what our personal heart habits of thinking, feeling, and living make us. And here is where identity theft turns spiritual, for it is in the spiritual realm that we find the devil and his evil angels specializing—railroading people through manifold temptations to keep us from experiencing God's ultimate identity exchange from the old sin-damaged person, scarred with damaging habits, to the new Christ-like creation of grace-empowered, faith-inspired victory, hope, and healing, which delights in visiting with God in praise-filled thankful prayer!

We considered, in the last chapter, that God's object in all His dealing with us is to lead us back to His original plan for mankind, which is to be like Him, developing a loving character like the one Jesus modeled for us while on earth (Romans 8:28, 29). And get this—before the dust of the great controversy between good and evil settles on planet earth and despite all the interference of the spiritual enemy, there will emerge a group of grace-empowered, faith-filled Christians who have come into such an intimate love relationship with Jesus Christ, through cooperation with the work of the Holy Spirit in their lives, that it will be said of them as Jesus said of Himself, *"the prince of this world cometh, and hath nothing in me"* (John 14:30, KJV; 1 John 2:5, 6; 3:2, 3). But how will this ever be accomplished? If we as Christians are honest with ourselves, most of us have struggled with some unhealthy besetting habit of life that seems nearly impossible to overcome. Well, here's the good news: *"There's nothing too hard for God"* to accomplish in our lives (Jeremiah 32:17; Luke 1:37) *if we are willing*— through faith, the empowering grace of God, and the word of His grace (Acts 20:32)—to diligently, determinedly, and consistently cooperate with the Holy Spirit in practicing saving belief, healing godly repentance, and thankful importunate prayer in a growing love relationship with Jesus Christ (John 14:23) through a continuing diligent faith-filled grace-empowered study and practice of God's Word (2 Timothy 2:15; James 1:22). The Bible uses several terms to speak of the ongoing Christian experience of physical, mental, and spiritual growth: (1) *sanctification* (1 Thessalonians 4:3, 7; 5:23; 2 Thessalonians 2:13,14), (2) *putting off the old man, putting on the new* (Ephesians 4:22–24; Colossians 3:9, 10), (3) *perfecting holiness* (2 Corinthians 7:1; Hebrews 12:14; 1 Peter 1:15), and (4) *purification* (1 John 3:2, 3). All these terms describe what I believe to be the most important identity exchange in all of human experience—the vital Spirit-inspired, grace-empowered work of replacing our old identity containing sin-damaged habits with our new Christ-like identity consisting of Christ-like habits of thinking and the responses that we were originally designed to joyfully experience for eternity (Philippians 2:5; 1 John 2:5, 6). Since we are what our thoughts make us (Proverbs 23:7), this godly exchange of identity entails the diligent practice of switching the focus of our attention away from self-centered thoughts to God-centered thoughts, as Jesus modeled for us, by exercising faith-engendered, grace-empowered choice. It is the miraculous renewal spoken of in Romans 12:2, *"And do not be conformed to this world, but be transformed by the renewing of your mind, that you may prove what is that good and acceptable and perfect will of God."*

This is what Jesus practiced throughout His sojourn here on earth all the way to His death on the cross of Calvary. We see it modeled in His open confrontation with Satan in the wilderness of temptation. (See chapter 3.) Catch Christ's model of dependence upon God the Father revealed in His words and actions:

"I can of Myself do nothing. As I hear, I judge; and My judgment is righteous, because I do not seek My own will but the will of the Father who sent Me." (John 5:30)

"For I have come down from heaven, not to do My own will, but the will of Him who sent Me." (John 6:38)

Jesus answered them and said, "My doctrine [teaching] is not Mine, but His who sent Me." (John 7:16)

Then Jesus said to them, "When you lift up the Son of Man, then you will know that I am He, and that I do nothing of Myself; but as My Father taught Me, I speak these things. And He who sent Me is with Me. The Father has not left Me alone, for I always do those things that please Him." (John 8:28, 29)

"For I have not spoken on My own authority; but the Father who sent Me gave Me a command, what I should say and what I should speak. And I know that His command is everlasting life. Therefore, whatever I speak, just as the Father has told Me, so I speak." (John 12:49, 50)

We see the epitome of Christ's prayer-filled, faith-engendered, grace-empowered identity as He surrendered in the Garden of Gethsemane, when, in great agony of heart, He sweat great drops of blood, carrying the guilt of all the sins of mankind. Then, knowing that He, an innocent victim, was going to be taken captive and crucified for us as a vile criminal, He spoke these words in prayer to His heavenly Father:

"Father, if it is Your will, take this cup away from Me; nevertheless not My will, but Yours, be done." (Luke 22:42)

We can be eternally thankful for the model of self-surrender, saving belief, godly thinking, and consecrated prayer that our Savior left for us in His life—a life that was crowned with heavenly glory in His death for you and me!

We can be eternally thankful for the model of self-surrender, saving belief, godly thinking, and consecrated prayer that our Savior left for us in His life—a life that was crowned with heavenly glory in His death for you and me!

Here is undeniable proof of the kind of victory that is possible for us in Christ, through faith-engendered, grace-empowered repentance, saving belief, and persevering prayer in surrender to God's will rather than in reliance on our own self-centered ways of coping. This, dear reader, is what the Lord

Jesus has for you and me versus what life on this sin-damaged planet offers us! Will you, by grace-empowered faith, choose to persistently practice true saving belief, true godly repentance, and diligent prayer, as you daily study God's Word to know Christ and His healing ways? You will be eternally grateful that you did—and truly UNBOUND! Courage! (See Philippians 1:6.)

Further Inspired Insight

The glory of God, the perfection of Christian character, is to be the aim, the purpose, of our life … *Like Christ* is the watchword, not like your father or your mother, but like Jesus Christ—hid in Christ, clothed with Christ's righteousness, imbued with the Spirit of Christ. (*Mind, Character, and Personality*, vol. 2, p. 643)

God's ideal for His children is higher than the highest human thought can reach. "Be ye therefore perfect, even as your Father which is in heaven is perfect." This command is a promise. The plan of redemption contemplates our complete recovery from the power of Satan. Christ always separates the contrite soul from sin. He came to destroy the works of the devil, and He has made provision that the Holy Spirit shall be imparted to every repentant soul, to keep him from sinning. (*The Desire of Ages*, p. 311)

We need a constant sense of the ennobling power of pure thoughts. The only security for any soul is right thinking. As a man "thinketh in his heart, so is he." Proverbs 23:7. The power of self-restraint strengthens by exercise. That which at first seems difficult, by constant repetition grows easy, until right thoughts and actions become habitual. If we will we may turn away from all that is cheap and inferior, and rise to a high standard; we may be respected by men and beloved of God. (*Ministry of Healing*, p. 491)

The religion of Christ is not what many think it is, nor what their lives represent it to be. The love of God in the soul will have a direct influence upon the life, and will call the intellect and the affections into active, healthful exercise. The child of God will not rest satisfied until he is clothed with the righteousness of Christ, and sustained by his life-giving power. When he sees a weakness in his character, it is not enough to confess it again and again; he must go to work with determination and energy to overcome his defects by building up opposite traits of character. He will not shun this work because it is difficult. Untiring energy is required of the Christian; but he is not obliged to work in his own strength; divine power awaits his demand. Every one who is sincerely striving for victory over self will appropriate the promise, "My grace is sufficient for thee."

Through personal effort joined with the prayer of faith, the soul is trained. Day by day the character grows into the likeness of Christ; and finally, instead of being the sport of circumstances, instead of indulging selfishness and being carried away by light and trifling conversation, the man is master of his thoughts and words. It may cost a severe conflict to overcome habits which have been long indulged, but we may triumph through the grace of Christ. He invites us to learn of him. (*Review and Herald*, June 10, 1884, alluding to Matthew 11:28–30)

Appendix

Components of victorious faith-engendered, grace-empowered saving belief and godly repentance:

1. Trustworthy information from God's Word (Psalm 12:6; 119:160; 2 Timothy 3:16, 17).

2. Faith-engendered, grace-empowered willingness to study the Bible daily to know God personally and to experience a godly change in heart motivation (John 17:3; 2 Corinthians 3:17, 18).

3. The ongoing faith-engendered, grace-empowered decision to practice exercising saving belief in God by:

   a. Trusting what God says in His Word

b. Thinking only what God says about the life circumstances that He allows me to experience.

c. Conversing with Him in thankful prayer using His Word as the focus of conversation.

4. The ongoing practice of true repentance to transform the old ways of thinking and responding to Christ's ways.

What is the fruit of such an experience? It is active participation in the works of Christ that we were created and re-created to experience—including the healing fruits of the Spirit, victory over the enemy's temptations, an ongoing practice of thankfulness for everything that God allows into our lives, the peace of God that passes all understanding, and the incontrovertible witness of His transforming character of love, power, and glory! (See Galatians 5:22, 23; Ephesians 2:8–10; 1 Corinthians 15:56–58; 1 Thessalonians 5:18; Philippians 4:4–8; Isaiah 43:10, 11; 2 Timothy 1:12; Revelation 4:11.) Christ Jesus assures us in John 8:31,32, "If you abide in My word, you are My disciples indeed. And you shall know the truth, and the truth shall make you free." Truly UNBOUND!